CliffsNotes™

A Doll's House & Hedda Gabler

By Marianne Sturman

IN THIS BOOK

- Introduction
- Biography of Ibsen
- Brief Summaries of Five Plays by Ibsen
- Act Summaries and Commentaries
- Critical Comments
- Character Analyses
- Selected Bibliography
- Selected Questions
- Find additional information to further your study online at www.cliffsnotes.com

WILEY

Wiley Publishin

Publisher's Acknowledgments

Editor
Gary Carey, M.A., University of Colorado

Consulting Editor
James L. Roberts, Ph.D., Department of
English, University of Nebraska

Composition
Wiley Indianapolis Composition Services

CliffsNotes™ *Ibsen's A Doll's House & Hedda Gabler*

Published by:
Wiley Publishing, Inc.
111 River Street
Hoboken, NJ 07030
www.wiley.com

CONTENTS

INTRODUCTION

Once the subject of public controversy, defended only by the *avant-garde* theater critics of the nineteenth century, Ibsen's prose dramas now appear as successful television plays and are an essential part of the repertory theaters all over the world. No longer inflaming audience reactions, the dramas are now acceptable fare to the most conservative theatergoer.

Because Ibsenite drama has become part of the history of the theater, a study of his work gives us a special insight into contemporary writings. The modern "theater of the absurd," for instance, expressing a personal alienation from society, is merely another form of the social criticism which Ibsen first inspired.

With this in mind, these synopses of Ibsen's *A Doll's House* and *Hedda Gabler* and their accompanying critical commentaries are designed to help the student rediscover the significance of Ibsen's work and to guide him in evaluating the contemporary appeal — if any — of his drama.

The purpose of these Notes is to amplify the student's understanding of the plays; by no means can this booklet substitute the esthetic and emotional satisfaction to be gained from reading the plays themselves. Because Ibsen's dramas lend themselves to a variety of interpretations, the student should feel encouraged to develop his own critical approach to Ibsen from reading this volume. Designed to encourage discussion between the student and the critic represented in this writing, the Notes should be merely used as a basis for a critical dialogue. The plays themselves must supply the intellectual stimulation.

A BRIEF BIOGRAPHY OF IBSEN

Henrick Ibsen's ancestors were sea captains and businessmen, while his father was a well-to-do merchant, dealing chiefly in lumber. Ibsen was born in 1828 in Skien, a town in the south of Norway. Three brothers and a sister were born after him, but Henrick was the only member of his family to show promise. When he was eight years old, his father's business failed and the family retired to a country house. Ibsen bitterly recalled how their friends, eager to dine and drink as guests of the affluent merchant, forsook all connections with the Ibsens when they lost their financial standing.

Although the young Ibsen showed talent as a painter, his family was too poor to allow him to study art; neither could they afford to train him for his chosen profession in medicine. When he was fifteen, his father sent him to Grimstad, a small provincial town south of Skien. Here he became an apothecary's apprentice, the next best thing to medicine. In the first three years of his Grimstad life, Ibsen lived entirely alone. Too uncommunicative to make friends and too poor to seek entertainments, he read voraciously, particularly in contemporary poetry and in theology. Eventually he was the center of a small circle of young men, and during this time began to write poetry.

Learning Latin in order to prepare for the university, Ibsen studied Cicero and became deeply interested in the character of Catiline, the agitator and revolutionary who was eventually assassinated. His first play, a historical drama in verse, was an attempt to explain this elusive character. *Catiline,* however, when published at the private expense of one enthusiastic friend, received no public notice and few copies were sold.

After six dark years in the hostile atmosphere of this provincial Norwegian village, Ibsen, by extreme economy and privation, had saved enough money to leave for the capital, Christiania (Oslo). Hoping to study at the university, he enrolled in a "student factory," a popular name given to an irregular school which coached students for the entrance examinations. Here Ibsen first met his lifelong rival and contemporary, Björnstjerne Björnson, who was to be known in the future, along with Ibsen, as a national poet of Norway. Found deficient in two subjects, Ibsen failed to enter the university. At this time as well, *Catiline* was rejected by the Christiania theater, but his *The Warrior's Barrow* was accepted and performed three times in 1850.

At this period of Ibsen's youth, Norway experienced a nationalist awakening. The new literary generation, after four hundred years of Danish rule (1397-1818), sought to revive the glories of Norwegian history and medieval literature. The middle ages were glorified as well because the romantic movement was in full swing throughout Europe. Thus, when Ole Bull, the great violinist, founded a Norse theater at Bergen, the project met with enthusiastic approval from all the youthful idealists eager to subvert the influence of Danish culture.

At a benefit performance to raise money for the new venture, Ibsen presented the prologue—a poem glorifying Norway's past—which moved Ole Bull to appoint him theater poet and stage manager of the Bergen theater. This position launched Ibsen on his dramatic career. Staging more than 150 plays, including works by Shakespeare and the French dramatist Scribe, Ibsen gained as much practical experience in stagecraft as that possessed by Shakespeare and Molière. In addition to his managerial position, the poet was obliged to produce one original play a year. Although his *The Warrior's Barrow* and *St. John's Night* met with failure, the critics approved of *Lady Inger of Östraat* (1855) and *The Feast at Solhaug* (1856). In this same year, the twenty-eight year old Ibsen became engaged to Susannah Thoresen, a girl of strong personality and independent judgment, and the marriage took place two years later.

Encouraged by the success of Ole Bull's Norse theater in Bergen, enthusiasts of nationalist poetry in the capital also founded a new theater in direct competition with the conservative, Danish-influenced Christiania Theater. Asked to direct this new venture, Ibsen's promised salary was twice the amount he received at Bergen, about six hundred specie dollars.

Returning to the capital with a new play, *The Vikings at Helgeland,* Ibsen first submitted the manuscript to the old Christiania Theater where he would be free to collect royalties. At first the Danish director accepted the piece, but returned it a few months later with a flimsy excuse. This gratuitous insult sparked a hot controversy between Ibsen, Björnson, and their followers on the one hand, and the adherents of the Danish influence on the other. After five years of public controversy, the conservative director was forced to resign, while *The Vikings* became one of the chief pieces performed under the theater's new management.

Throughout these early years, the relationship between Ibsen and Björnson was very friendly. Björnson became godfather when the Ibsens' son, Sigurd, was born in 1859; when the dramatist was in serious financial straits, Björnson made every effort to raise money for him. The two men also shared the same circle of friends at this time, although Ibsen was disappointed to find that his poetic ideals were misunderstood by his gregarious contemporaries. In a poem, *On the Heights,* he expressed the view that a man who wishes to devote himself to the arts must sacrifice the usual pleasures of life; a poet must view life apart in order to find in it models for his work.

Ibsen suffered great depression during this part of his life. The varied responsibilities of his job allowed him no chance for his own creative work. In addition, the theater was doing so badly that his salary was severely reduced. Besides neglecting his work, he published no play from 1857 until *Love's Comedy* in 1862. This new anti-romantic satire received hostile reviews although it shows a maturing talent and the bold viewpoint which characterizes his later works. When the theater finally declared bankruptcy, Ibsen's despair was complete. Like Captain Alving, he became a victim of that "second-rate town which had no joys to offer—only dissipations," and spent much time in barrooms. Björnson, meanwhile, was a successful and already famous poet to whom the government awarded an annual grant of four hundred dollars to devote himself exclusively to poetic works. However Ibsen's fortunes changed in the following year when *The Pretenders,* a play glorifying the Norse heroes of the past, won an enthusiastic reception from both audience and reviewers. As a result of this success, the government awarded Ibsen a travelling scholarship to bring him in contact with the cultural trends in the rest of Europe.

Visiting Rome, Ibsen viewed for the first time the great art masterpieces of the classical and renaissance periods. In the warm, sunny climate of Italy, Ibsen felt intoxicated with his freedom from the stultifying atmosphere of Norwegian provincialism. Retiring with his family to a little town in the hills, Ibsen wrote with an inspired pen. Affected by the events of the Prusso-Danish war over Schleswig-Holstein, his interests turning from the esthetic to the ethical, Ibsen produced the colossal *Brand*.

Considered "the most stirring event in Norway's literary history of the nineteenth century," this drama won nationwide fame for its composer. The protagonist of the play, a mystical clergyman, is a courageous idealist of noble stature whose lack of love or humanity destroys his own wife and child in an uncompromising commitment to his ethical principles.

Published in the following year, *Peer Gynt* established Ibsen's international fame. This exuberant, fantasy-filled drama is the antithesis of *Brand*. The spoiled darling of a weak mother and rich father, Peer lives according to the principle of "to thyself—enough." Rather than overcoming obstacles, he goes "roundabout" and avoids facing problems. Unlike Brand, Peer never commits himself to principles unless they are to his personal benefit. The play is full of symbolic allusions and rich lyrical poetry. In 1867, the king decorated Ibsen for his achievement.

After four years in Italy, Ibsen settled down to his lifework, first in Dresden and then in Munich. His biography from this point on is more or less uneventful. Producing a new play every two years, Ibsen's dramatic powers increased and his social criticism ripened. Along with Björnson, he was considered Norway's greatest poet, but he maintained primacy as a dramatist. Honors heaped upon him and with a prosperous income, Ibsen appeared as a frock-coated and respectable middle class individual.

Almost entirely self-inspired, Ibsen was a rare genius who required no outside influence for his work. Unlike Björnson who lectured, made frequent public appearances and wrote novels and plays as well as poems, Ibsen kept to himself as much as possible. Constantly working and reworking his dramas throughout each two year period, rarely divulging, even to his family, the nature of his current writing, he single-mindedly pursued his art. Just as he gave up painting in his youth for writing poetry and drama, he now stopped composing poems, eventually relinquishing even the verse form of his earlier plays for the prose of the later works.

Harsh self-analysis was one of his life principles. In each play he expresses this constant introspection, always underscoring a thesis based on self-seeking. In *Emperor and Galilean,* for example, Julian fails to establish the "first empire" of pagan sensuality, then casts aside the "second empire" of Christian self-abnegation. As the hero expires, he envisions a "third empire," where, in the words of the biographer Zucker, "men were to find God not on Mount Olympus nor on Calvary but in their own souls, wills, and senses." Ibsen himself once wrote in a poem, that "to live is to fight with trolls in heart and brain. To be a poet is to pronounce a final judgment upon oneself."

The Norwegian commentator Francis Bull (1887–1974) sums up Ibsen's personal search:

> More deeply than ordinary men, Ibsen was split in two — a great genius and a shy and timid little philistine. In daily life he quite often did not come up to his own heroic ideals and revolutionary theories, but listened to the troll voices of narrow-minded egotism and compromise — and then, afterwards, the genius in him arose, a judge without mercy. This ever-recurring fight meant to him lifelong suffering; but it was this drama constantly going on in his own soul that made him a great dramatist and compelled him again and again to undertake a penetrating self-analysis.

Ibsen died in 1906. His tombstone, inscribed only with a hammer, the miner's symbol, alludes to a poem Ibsen wrote as a youth. Ending with "Break me the way, you heavy hammer,/To the deepest bottom of my heart," the verse is a succinct statement of the intensity of Ibsen's personal vision and of his dramatic art.

FIVE PLAYS BY IBSEN: A BRIEF SUMMARY

Ibsen's most famous plays include *A Doll's House, Ghosts, An Enemy of the People, The Wild Duck,* and *Hedda Gabler.* For the analysis of the plays not included in this volume, see the companion volume on Ibsen in "Cliff's Notes."

A DOLL'S HOUSE

Norma Helmer once secretly borrowed a large sum of money so that her husband could recuperate from a serious illness. She never told him of this loan and has been secretly paying it back in small installments by saving from her household allowance. Her husband, Torvald, thinks her careless and childlike, and often calls her his doll. When he is appointed bank director, his first act is to relieve a man who was once disgraced for having forged his signature on a document. This man, Nils Krogstad, is the person from whom Nora has borrowed her money. It is then revealed that she forged her father's signature in order to get the money. Krogstad threatens to reveal Nora's crime and thus disgrace her and her husband unless Nora can convince her husband not to fire him. Nora tries to influence her husband, but he thinks of Nora as a simple child who cannot understand the value of money or business. Thus, when Helmer discovers that Nora has forged her father's name, he is ready to disclaim his wife even though she had done it for him. Later when all is solved, Nora sees that her husband is not worth her love and she leaves him.

HEDDA GABLER

Hedda, the famous daughter of General Gabler, married George Tesman out of desperation. But she found life with him to be dull and tedious. During their wedding trip, her husband spent most of his time in libraries doing research in history for a book that is soon to be published. He is hoping to receive a position in the university.

An old friend of Hedda's comes to visit her and tells her of Eilert Lovborg, an old friend of both women. Eilert Lovborg has also written a book on history that is highly respected. In the past, however, he has lived a life of degeneration. Now he has quit drinking and has devoted himself to serious work. His new book has all the imagination and spirit that is missing in George Tesman's book. Hedda's friend, Thea Elvsted, tells how she has helped Eilert stop drinking and begin constructive work.

Later at a visit, Lovborg is offered a drink. He refuses and Hedda, jealous over the influence that Thea has on Lovborg, tempts him into taking a drink. He then goes to a party where he loses his manuscript. When George Tesman returns home with Lovborg's manuscript, Hedda burns it because she is jealous of it. Later, Lovborg comes to her and confesses how he has failed in his life. Hedda talks him into committing suicide by shooting himself in the temple. Lovborg does commit suicide later but it is through a wound in the stomach. George then begins to reconstruct Lovborg's manuscript with the help of notes provided by Thea Elvsted. Suddenly, Hedda leaves the room, takes her pistols and commits suicide.

GHOSTS

Mrs. Alving is building an orphanage as a memorial to her husband. This edifice is to be dedicated the next day, and her old friend Parson Manders has come to perform the ceremonies. In a private conversation, Mrs. Alving tells the Parson that her husband had been a complete degenerate, and she is using the rest of his money to build the orphanage so that she can leave *only* her money to her son Oswald, who has just arrived home from years and years abroad.

In a private talk with his mother, Oswald confesses that he has an incurable disease which the doctors think was inherited. Oswald, however, believes his father to have been a perfect man. Mrs. Alving, then, must confess that Mr. Alving had indeed been a degenerated man and that Oswald caught the disease from his father. Oswald knows that he is dying and wants to take the maid as his mistress so that the maid, Regina, will give him poison when he is next struck by the disease. Mrs. Alving then explains that Regina is in reality his half sister. This does not bother Oswald, but Regina refuses to stay. Oswald then tells his mother that she must administer the medicine when the next attack comes. As the play closes, Oswald begins to have his attack and his mother does not know whether to administer the poison or to endure the agony.

AN ENEMY OF THE PEOPLE

Dr. Stockmann has discovered that the new baths built in his town are infected with a deadly disease and instructs the town to repair or close the baths. The mayor, who is Dr. Stockmann's brother, does not believe the report and refuses to close the baths because it will cause the financial ruin of the town.

Dr. Stockmann tries to take his case to the people, but the mayor intercedes and explains to the people how much it will cost to repair the baths. He explains that the doctor is always filled with wild, fanciful ideas. In a public meeting, he has his brother declared an enemy of the people. The doctor decides to leave the town, but at the last minute comes to the realization that he must stay and fight for the things he believes to be right.

THE WILD DUCK

Gregers Werle has avoided his father, whom he detests, by spending fifteen years in the family mining concern. Gregers is so unattractive in appearance that he has given up all hope of marrying and having a family; instead, he has become an idealist and goes about advocating and preaching a theme of truth and purity. He calls his mission the "claim of the ideal."

His father, Old Werle, has allegedly driven his sick wife to her death by carrying on love affairs in his own home. He had once had his serving girl, Gina, as his mistress. Arranging her marriage with Hialmar Ekdal, the son of his former partner, Werle also sets the couple up in the profession of photography. Hialmar is pleased with his marriage and believes that Gina's child is his own daughter. At present, Old Werle lives with his housekeeper and between them there are no secrets.

Lieutenant Ekdal, Werle's former partner, is now a broken old man. He does odd jobs for Werle. Earlier, the company had appropriated a large quantity of lumber from a government-owned farm. Werle placed all the blame on Ekdal who was sentenced to prison. He is now living with Hialmar and Gina.

Gregers Werle comes to Hialmar and explains the claim of the ideal and tries to make Hialmar see that his marriage is based on a lie. But rather than making Hialmar happy by understanding the true nature of his marriage, Gregers only succeeds in turning Hialmar against his daughter, Hedvig. The daughter, in order to prove her love for her father who is rejecting her, takes a pistol and kills herself. Hialmar then becomes bitterly remorseful about his behavior.

A DOLL'S HOUSE

ACT I

Summary

Very cheerful, the pretty and girlish Nora Helmer enters from the outdoors, humming a tune while she deposits her parcels on the hall table. "Is that my little lark twittering out there?" calls her husband from the study, and he emerges to greet her. They talk about their improved income because Torvald has just been appointed as bank manager, and Nora chatters about Christmas presents she has just purchased for the children. Helmer suspects that his "Miss Sweet Tooth" has been "breaking rules" by indulging herself in prohibited confection. Nora denies the accusation, but the audience has seen her pop macaroons in her mouth as she came in. Deftly, Nora changes the subject and talks about decorating the tree.

The maid tells Torvald that their family friend, Dr. Rank, awaits him in his room. When Helmer has gone, another visitor arrives to see Nora, and the two women, who have not seen each other for the past ten years, are alone onstage. Christine Linde, having just returned to her home town, tells Nora all about her unfortunate life. Married unlovingly, widowed for the past three years, Mrs. Linde experienced the hardships of a woman who was forced to make her own way. She points out that her toilsome life has aged her, while

Nora is as innocent and childlike as ever. Nora declares that she too has worked and sacrificed all these years. Her toil has saved someone she loves, she boasts, and she tells Christine how she borrowed 250 pounds when Torvald's health was in such danger that he needed to go to a southern climate to improve his condition. She describes how she secretly repaid installments of the debt by stinting on her personal expenses and taking in copying work to do at night. Mrs. Linde is amazed that Nora has not mentioned the matter to her husband in all these years. He would never consent to borrowing money, Nora explains, and involuntarily she exposes the real reason for the deception: to save face for Helmer.

> How painful and humiliating it would be for Torvald, with his manly independence, to know that he owed me anything [says Nora]. It would upset our mutual relations altogether; our beautiful happy home would no longer be what it is now.

Mrs. Linde, still amazed, asks if Nora will ever reveal her secret to Helmer. Some day she shall, answers the girl with a half-smile. It may be good to "have something in reserve" in future years when she is no longer as attractive as now, "when my dancing and dressing-up and reciting have palled on him," Nora says.

The maid announces another visitor for Torvald. The newcomer, Nils Krogstad, is a lawyer and moneylender who now works at the bank. Nora seems relieved when he says he has come merely to talk with Helmer about "dry business matters." Leaving the study to allow Krogstad a private talk with his chief, Dr. Rank emerges to greet the ladies. Obsessed with thoughts of illness, the physician characterizes Krogstad as "morally diseased." Like many of his physically diseased patients, he continues, the lawyer refuses to submit to his fate, despite great agony, in the hopes of a change in his position.

This idea draws a parallel between Krogstad's situation and that of Dr. Rank. The lawyer feels his job is threatened now that Helmer is his chief, while Rank, ill with a congenital disease, is close to losing his life. With this in mind, Ibsen indicates that Krogstad clings to his respectability, or moral health, just as Dr. Rank clings to whatever physical life he has left.

Now that he has dismissed his visitor, Torvald emerges from the study and meets Mrs. Linde for the first time. Recommending that Helmer find a job for Christine, Nora makes up a little story to push her point. Her friend rushed to town, the wife relates, just as soon as she heard of Helmer's promotion in hopes of finding a place at the bank. "She is frightfully anxious to work under some clever man so as to perfect herself," concludes Nora despite Mrs. Linde's remonstrances."Very sensible," approves Torvald, and with a well-favored "we'll see what we can do" he resumes his visit with Rank in the study. Now that Mrs. Linde has left to seek lodgings, Nora admits the nurse and loudly greets her three children.

During the noisy romp, Nora crawls under the table to play hide and seek. She emerges growling and the children shriek with laughter. No one has heard Krogstad's knock on the door. He enters, and when Nora emerges from under the table again, she gives a stifled cry at discovering her villain. Ushering the children out of the room, Nora is alone with Krogstad.

He has come, he says, to ask her to intercede with Helmer on his behalf for only her influence can protect the job which Christine Linde might take from him. He tells her that, for the sake of his growing sons, he has been working to restore his fallen position in society and he is prepared to fight for this small post in the bank as if he were "fighting for his life." Nora shows little interest until he says he is able to compel her to comply with his request. Krogstad reveals that he can prove she borrowed the 250 pounds from him by forging her father's signature. Her situation was desperate when she needed the money, Nora explains. Her father, who died soon afterward, was too ill at the time to be consulted about such matters. Surely it is no crime for a woman to do everything possible to save her husband's life, Nora declares. Forgery is a criminal act, Krogstad reminds her, and the law cares nothing about motivation. He tells her that the one false step in his own life, the one that ruined his reputation and his career "was nothing more nor nothing worse than what you have done." This is Nora's first confrontation with the harsh inflexibility of lawful society. For the last time, Krogstad asks Nora to help him keep his post. If necessary, he says, he would produce the forged bond in court. His parting words frighten Nora and she tries to distract herself by considering her Christmas decorations.

Interrupting her thoughts, Torvald comes to ask what Krogstad wanted. He is angry at Nora's evasive answer, but she finally admits that the lawyer begged her to say a good word in his behalf. Torvald becomes agreeable after Nora coaxes him to be her supervisor in choosing her costume for the fancy dress party they are to attend the next evening. Then she slowly leads the talk back to Krogstad. He once committed a forgery, Helmer tells her. "Out of necessity?" asks Nora, and he nods. Any man is allowed one false move, Torvald continues, so long as he openly confesses and accepts his punishment. But Krogstad, by his cunning, avoided the consequences of his guilt.

> Just think [says Helmer] how a guilty man like that has to lie and play the hypocrite with everyone, how he has to wear a mask in the presence of those near and dear to him, even before his own wife and children. And about the children, that is the most terrible part.

He goes on to describe how "infection and poison" pollutes the very atmosphere breathed in such a home. While Nora becomes increasingly agitated, Torvald continues his lecture. In his career as a lawyer, her husband affirms, he has discovered that everyone who has "gone bad early in life" had a deceitful mother, since it is she whose influence dictates the children's moral character. He leaves Nora, stunned with horror at his words. When the nurse enters with the children she refuses to see them. "No, no, no! Don't let them come in to me," Nora pleads. It can't possibly be true, she says to herself, "Deprave my little children? Poison my home?" She is pale with terror at her thoughts while the curtain descends.

Commentary

By the end of this first act, Nora is emerging from the protection of her married life to confront the conditions of the outside world. Although she has been content in being a protected and cared-for housewife during the past eight years, and has once averted a crisis by finding a way to borrow money for the sake of Torvald's health, Nora has never learned to overtly challenge her environment.

Mrs. Linde, on the other hand, has independently faced life's challenge, although she too sought protection by marrying for the sake of financial convenience. Her harsh experience as a widow who was forced to earn her own livelihood stands in sharp contrast to the insulated and frivolous life which Nora leads. Having learned, through suffering, the value of truthful human relationships, Christine is the first person to recognize that Nora's marriage is based on deception.

The device Ibsen uses to describe the Helmer's dece_ . ·e marital relationship is the problem of Nora's debt. To prevent Torvald from discovering her secret, he shows how Nora has developed the manner of an evasive, charming adolescent whose whims and caprices her grown-up husband must indulge. This bolsters Torvald's self-image as a protector of the weak, the head of a dependent household, and the instructor of the mentally inferior.

The audience is immediately aware of Torvald's shallowness as he utters his first condescending words to his wife. Nora herself provides further evidence: when she says that Helmer might one day tire of her "reciting and dressing-up and dancing" she unknowingly describes the decadence of her marital relationship. Pedantic and pompous, Torvald sometimes seems like a father who enjoys the innocence of a favorite daughter. Setting up rules of behavior (prohibiting Nora's macaroons, for instance), instructing his wife even in her very dress, Helmer shows that he regards her as a plaything or a pet rather than an independent person. These attitudes suggest the baldly sexual nature of Helmer's marriage; the theme is later expanded in following acts until Nora recognizes her position and finds her role repulsive as well as humiliating.

Krogstad shows Nora another deceptive quality about the nature of the world: an individual is responsible for his own acts. Society punishes its lawbreaker; the innocent wife acting to save the life of her loved one is equally as guilty as the unscrupulous opportunist who acts out of expediency. Once recognizing the parallel between the "morally diseased" Krogstad and herself, Nora begins to confront the realities of the world and with this new knowledge she must draw the inevitable conclusions.

ACT II

Summary
It is later in the same day. Nora has avoided her children, fearing to pollute them. In a conversation with her old nurse, she tells the servant that the children will have to get used to seeing less of their mother from now on. This is Nora's first suggestion of withdrawing from the life she has lived up until now.

While Nora unpacks her costume from the box—the Italian fisher girl dress which reminds Torvald of their Italian honeymoon trip—Mrs. Linde enters and busies herself in sewing a tear in the garment. They discuss Dr. Rank and Christine is shocked by Nora's knowledge of inherited disease, a subject usually shielded from innocent ears. Being herself far from naive, she reproaches Nora for having borrowed the money from Dr. Rank to pay for Helmer's rest cure in Italy. Emphatically the girl denies it, for, she says, she would never allow herself placed in such a "horribly painful position" toward their old friend.

Helmer's appearance interrupts the conversation. Nora goes to greet him, and then, very prettily, coaxes her husband once more to allow Krogstad to keep his position in the bank. Nora says she is afraid he might write malicious slander about Torvald in the newspapers, threatening his new position just as her father had once been threatened. This is the part of their dialogue which illuminates the character and circumstances of Nora's father who was once a government official. Sent by the department to investigate the truth of the newspaper charges against her father, Helmer cleared his name; as a conquering hero he then married the grateful daughter.

Helmer admits that Krogstad's moral failings can be overlooked, but he is most annoyed at the moneylender's embarrassingly familiar manner toward him when there are other people around. Because they were once intimate friends, Krogstad presumes familiarity and by this attitude, Torvald says, "he would make my position in the bank intolerable." Nora is surprised, and insults Helmer by remarking how unlike him it is to take such "a narrowminded way of looking at things." He is so peeved at her estimation that he calls the maid to immediately post the letter of Krogstad's dismissal.

"Call her back, Torvald, Do you hear me, call her back," Nora pleads in panic. Taking her in his arms, he says he is not afraid of a "starving quilldriver's vengeance." Whatever happens, Helmer declares, "you may be sure that I am man enough to take everything upon myself." Nora reads much more meaning into this. "You will never have to do that," she vows. Alone onstage, Nora desperately thinks of some way to pay off the last part of the debt and free herself from Krogstad.

At this point, Dr. Rank arrives. He has come, he says, to tell her that he has one more month left to live. When the final "horrors of dissolution" begin, he will send her a card marked with a black cross for he intends to remain alone like a sick animal when it is time to die. A victim of tuberculosis of the spine, Rank denounces the "inexorable retribution" that innocent children must pay for their parent's excesses, and Nora covers her ears to prevent hearing the references to her own life and her own children.

To avoid the serious talk, Nora chatters about her dress, flirtatiously showing Rank her silk stockings. The doctor becomes serious again, expressing sorrow at being unable to leave her a token of gratitude for the friendship he enjoyed in this house. Nora, about to ask him to lend her money as a "big proof of friendship," never makes her request, for Rank responds to her hint with a passionate declaration of love. Nora rises, and quietly calls the servant to bring them more light.

As their conversation continues in the brightened room, she lapses into her former friendliness. Rank points out that she seems even more relaxed in his company than with Helmer. Nora explains that "there are some people one loves best and others whom one would almost always rather have as companions." When living with Papa, she used to steal into the maids' rooms because "they never moralized at all and talked to each other about such interesting things." She concludes with unconscious significance that "being with Torvald is a little like being with Papa."

At this point, the maid hands her Krogstad's visiting card. Finding some pretext, Nora excuses herself from Dr. Rank and confronts the moneylender who has just received Torvald's letter of dismissal. Krogstad informs Nora that he has no further interest in the money and he will keep the bond in a gesture of blackmail. With this weapon he will have the power to make Helmer guarantee his employment at the bank and to eventually attain a higher position.

Nora declares that her husband would never submit to such humiliation and hints she would rather sacrifice her life than have Torvald suffer blame for her crime. She is sure his protective nature would make him assume all the guilt, but Krogstad has a much lower opinion of Torvald's character. Turning to go, he tells her that he is leaving a letter informing Helmer of the forgery. Nora listens breathlessly as the footsteps pass downstairs. As they pause, she hears something drop into the letterbox; then the steps gradually diminish.

Returning to Christine, Nora tells of the forgery and the letter. She begs her friend to act as a witness "if anything should happen to me." Were someone to take all the blame, all the responsibility Christine must "remember that I alone did the whole thing." With mounting emotion, Nora says, "A wonderful thing is going to happen. But it is so terrible, Christine, it mustn't happen, not for all the world." Mrs. Linde insists upon paying Krogstad a visit right away. On the strength of their past love, she will ask him to recall the letter.

Torvald is accustomed at this hour to read his mail, and Nora tries to distract him. She tells him that she is so nervous about dancing the tarantella for the party that he must help her practice until the last minute. Agreeing to do nothing but instruct her dancing — not even open his mail — Torvald watches as Nora begins her dance, Rank playing the piano accompaniment. Despite her husband's instructions, Nora moves more and more violently, dancing "as if her life depended on it." Helmer suddenly cries "Stop! This is sheer madness. You have forgotten everything I've taught you." He embraces his nervous wife, suspecting that she is afraid of a letter Krogstad may have written. He promises not to look in the letterbox. "The child shall have her way," murmurs the comforting amorous husband. "But tomorrow night after you have danced — " "Then you will be free," she answers significantly.

Christine returns and tells Nora that Krogstad is out of town, but she left a letter for him. Alone, Nora resigns herself to suicide, reckoning that, until the end of the party, she has thirty-one hours left to live. "Where's my little skylark?" calls Helmer returning from the dining room to fetch her. As Nora stretches her arms out to him, the curtain falls.

Commentary

In this act, Nora learns that she alone must face the consequences of her guilt. Refusing to allow Torvald to take the blame, she prepares to kill herself.

The theme of death in this scene suggests a parallel between Nora and Dr. Rank, for the knowledge of his death coincides with her decision to commit suicide. Her tarantella is then a symbolic death dance which Rank, fittingly, plays for her on the piano. At the same time, since Helmer has chosen her dance costume to be that of a Capri fisher girl, the tarantella symbolizes their wedding, for Nora and Torvald learned the dance while honeymooning in Italy. Her dancing will be her final mortal performance, for Nora views the end of the party not only as the termination of her marriage, but as the last moments of her life.

The scene between Nora and Dr. Rank is a significant one. Not only does it underscore the "pollution and infection" which a guilty parent can pass on to his children — Nora being the guilt-ridden parent, Rank the victim of veneral disease — but it shows the youthful innocence of Nora. Accustomed to approaching her husband in a mood of adolescent flirtatiousness, Nora treats Dr. Rank the same way, as she shows him her leg dressed in the new silk stockings. When Rank responds with a declaration of love instead of amused paternity, Nora recognizes for the first time the underlying sexual nature of her relationship with Torvald. This sudden understanding prevents her asking Dr. Rank for the "big proof of friendship" which she would have been able to accept innocently from a family friend. Knowing that receiving payment from a lover places one in a "horribly painful position" reminds Nora how she has always cajoled Helmer to give her little presents of money. With this understanding, she begins to recognize how Torvald, regarding her as a romantic object, violates her personal independence.

Nora learns more about Torvald's weakness of character in this act, although she does not realize the full significance of this insight until the following scene. When Helmer tells her that he wishes to get rid of Krogstad, not because he judges him morally incompetent, but because he is ashamed to admit friendship with a man held to be disreputable, Nora observes that Torvald is quite different from the moralizing and respectable husband she has admired for eight years. Despite this insight, she still believes, as she tells Christine, that the "wonderful thing" will still take place—the proud terrible moment when Torvald discovers the forgery and takes all the guilt upon himself.

ACT III

Summary
Krogstad and Mrs. Linde are alone onstage, for the Helmers and Dr. Rank are upstairs at the masquerade party. Bitterly Krogstad reproaches Christine for renouncing their betrothal, years ago, sacrificing him in order to marry a man better able to support her and her family. After wrecking his hopes the first time, she appears again to stand in his way by taking over his hard-won position at the bank. Christine denies the charge. She says she returned to town to seek him and renew their love. Krogstad, deeply moved, is grateful for her love and faith. He says he will ask Helmer to return his letter, but Christine has changed her mind. Helmer must find out the truth, she says; all this concealment and falsehood must be exposed in order for Nora and Torvald to realize a true marriage.

After Krogstad has gone, Helmer enters, drawing Nora into the room while she struggles and protests that she wants to remain at the party a little longer. He is annoyed to find Mrs. Linde waiting up for them, and while he fetches candles, Christine tells Nora of her talk with Krogstad and counsels that "you must tell your husband all about it." With quiet resolve Nora answers, "Now I know what I must do."

Helmer is relieved when Christine finally leaves them alone. Flushed with champagne and romantic desires, he tells Nora that all this night "I have longed for nothing but you." Unable to endure his desire after watching her dance, he dragged her home. Nora twists out of his embrace. Before he can be angry, Dr. Rank enters to wish them good night, and Nora quickly senses the real reason for his visit. Turning to go, Rank says good-bye with unmistakable finality. "Sleep well," says Nora gently, adding, to his surprise, "Wish me the same."

To Nora's dismay, Torvald now goes to the letterbox. Dr. Rank has left them a visiting card marked with black; "as if he were announcing his own death," murmurs Helmer. After Nora tells him of Rank's condition, he clasps her tightly. Now that their closest friend is gone, he says, they must hold on to each other even more closely. "Do you know, Nora [Torvald whispers] I have often wished that you might be threatened by some great danger, so that I might risk my life's blood and everything for your sake."

She firmly disengages herself. "Now you must read your letters, Torvald," Nora declares. In deference to their friend's death, Torvald agrees to retire to his own room. Alone, Nora prepares to rush out to meet her own death "in the icy depths." Ready to leave her house, she gains the hall when Helmer meets her at the door of his room brandishing the letter. "You shan't save me, Torvald," cries Nora, struggling from him. In a paroxysm of self-pity and indignation, Helmer struts and shouts, vulgarly abusing his wife for bringing this shame upon him, for putting him into Krogstad's power. People might even suspect that he was responsible for the whole thing, that he prompted Nora to do the deed. At all costs the matter must be hushed up, Krogstad must be pacified. He renounces Nora as his wife. Although for the sake of appearance, she may still live in the house, she will not be allowed to raise the children and shall share no intimacy with her husband. Nora's answers are quieter and colder as Helmer talks.

Suddenly a maid, half-dressed, brings Nora a letter. Torvald grabs it, tears it open. A moment later he shouts with joy, "I am saved, Nora! I am saved," and he tears the enclosed bond into small pieces. Exultantly he forgives his wife, repeating all the platitudes he has always uttered about the cozy home he has with his skylark. "Here I will protect you like a hunted dove that I have saved from a hawk's claws," and he goes on to say, that by freely forgiving and accepting her once more as his own he has recreated his wife, giving her a new life.

By this time Nora has changed her party dress and appears in everyday clothes. "Sit down, Torvald," she says, "You and I have much to say to each other." Helmer shows surprise. "Nora, this cold set face — what is this?" Confronting her husband across a table, Nora proceeds to the "settling of accounts." First of all, she says, this is the first time in eight years "that we two, you and I, husband and wife, have had a serious conversation...We have never sat down in earnest together to try and get at the bottom of things." Over Torvald's sputtered objections she outlines the life she has been living in the "doll's house."

First she lived with her father who treated her as a toy, whose opinions and tastes she followed because he would be displeased with any disagreement, any sign of independence. "He played with me just as I used to play with my dolls. And when I came to live with you I was simply transferred from Papa's hands to yours." Torvald made all the arrangements in their life, she goes on to say, and so she never developed her own tastes or her own ideas.

When I look back on it, it seems to me as if I have been living here like a poor woman — just from hand to mouth. I have existed merely to perform tricks for you, Torvald. But you would have it so. You and Papa have committed a great sin against me. It is your fault I have made nothing of my life.

Helmer is forced to admit of some truth — though "strained and exaggerated" — in what she says. It shall be different in the future, he vows, "playtime shall be over and lesson time shall begin." She answers that he is not the man to educate her into being a proper wife. Neither is she ready to bring up her children, Nora continues, for there is another task she must first undertake. "I must try and educate myself," she says, "and I must do that for myself." That is why she is leaving him now. Finding her husband a stranger, Nora chooses to seek lodging with Christine rather than spend another night with him. Torvald points out that she has no right to neglect her most sacred duties — duties to her husband and children.

NORA: I have other duties just as sacred. Duties to myself.

HELMER: Before all else you are a wife and mother.

NORA: I don't believe that any longer, I believe that before all else I am a reasonable human being just as you are — or, at all events, that I must try and become one. I know quiet well, Torvald, that most people would think you right and that views of that kind are to be found in books; but I can no longer content myself with what most people say or with what is found in books. I must think over things for myself and get to understand them.

Torvald accuses her of loving him no longer. She nods, explaining that tonight "when the wonderful thing did not happen, then I saw you were not the man I had thought you." For such a long time she suffered with the guilty secret of her borrowed money, feeling certain that eventually the "wonderful thing" would happen. The chance came with Krogstad's letter, for Nora never imagined Torvald could submit to that man's conditions. She expected him to say proudly, "publish the thing to the whole world," and come forward to take the guilt upon himself. This expected sacrifice was the "wonderful thing" she had awaited, and to prevent it, she planned suicide.

Helmer says he is willing to toil for her day and night, bear any suffering, "but no man would sacrifice his honor for the one he loves." "It is a thing hundreds of thousands of women have always done," Nora quietly points out. She tells him that after his fear was over—"not the fear for what threatened me, but for what might happen to you"—and she became once more his little skylark, his doll, whose fragility demanded "doubly gentle care" in the future, she then realized that for eight years "I had been living with a strange man and had borne him three children." She cannot bear to think of this humiliation, Nora says, and will leave him without accepting money to live on and without communicating.

Torvald begs her to say when they can live together again. Nora sighs. "Ah, Torvald, the most wonderful thing of all would have to happen," she answers. They must both be so changed that "our life together would be a real wedlock." She turns to go, leaving Helmer, face in hands, repeating her name. Then he rises as a hope flashes across his mind. "The most wonderful thing of all—?" he murmurs. There is a noise of a door slamming shut.

Commentary

Clearly explaining the reasons for her sudden departure, Nora summarizes the entire play during her last speeches with Helmer. Discovering that her husband confuses appearance with values, that he is more concerned with his position in society than with the emotional needs of his wife, Nora is forced to confront her personal worthlessness. Rather than remain part of a marriage based on an intolerable lie, she chooses to leave her home and discover for herself the individuality which life with Helmer has denied her.

Central to this act, and in fact to the whole play, is Nora's concept of the "wonderful thing," the moment when she and Torvald would achieve a "real wedlock." In the course of the drama, she has learned that the ideal union takes place when husband and wife regard each other as rational individuals who are aware of society's demands and can fulfill their separate responsibilities with sophistication and mutual respect.

In another sense, the "wonderful thing" is merely a code word for a relationship whose values are freed from the mystique which society has attached to marriage with concept like "duty," "respectability," "cozy home," "happy family," and the rest of the stereotyped images such phrases suggest. A "real wedlock" can only be attained when a couple, deeply committed to respect each other's personal worth, work naturally and thoughtfully to fulfill ideals which their separate individualities require. Helmer, by striving for goals which have been thrust upon him in the course of an education based on social morality and verbal commitment to goals empty of feeling or commitment, deprives Nora of her sense of identity. To discover the essence of personal truth is then, the "wonderful thing" which Nora Helmer, unable to find in her marriage, must seek through her own resources.

GENERAL ANALYSIS OF *A DOLL'S HOUSE*

DRAMATIC STRUCTURE

Notable for their lack of action, Ibsen's dramas are classical in their staticism. Before the curtain rises, all the significant events have already occurred in the lives of Ibsen's characters, and it is the business of the play to reap the consequences of these past circumstances. The tight logical construction of each drama is the most important factor for the play's plausibility. With this in mind, Ibsen shows how every action of each character is the result of carefully detailed experiences in the earlier life of the person, whether in childhood, education, or genetic environment.

The author shows, for instance, that Nora's impetuosity and carelessness with money are qualities inherited from her father. Krogstad suddenly turns respectable because he needs to pass on a good name for the sake of his maturing sons. Mrs. Linde returns to town in order to renew her relationship with Krogstad. Finally, to account for Nora's secrecy with regard to the borrowed money, Ibsen shows how Torvald's way of life is devoted to maintaining appearances at the expense of inner truth.

CHARACTERS

To construct each drama even more tightly, Ibsen provides complex relationships among all his characters so that their weaknesses and strengths are reinforced by comparisons with others. Even a minor character, such as the old nurse, is significant, for she used to be Nora's nurse after the death of the girl's mother. The nurse, moreover, functions to assure the audience that Nora's children will be well-cared for in her absence, just as Nora herself was raised when her mother died. By bringing up this point early in the play, the dramatist forewarns the audience of Nora's suicide or her leaving home.

Christine Linde, Nora Helmer's contemporary, serves as a direct comparison with Ibsen's heroine. By recounting how she denied her rights to love and self-determination, by marrying for financial security, Mrs. Linde foreshadows how Nora will confront a bitter future after learning that her marriage is based on deception. Nora, according to Mrs. Linde's example, must eventually conclude, through her own sufferings, that the only way of life which can survive crises is one based on truthful relationships. The ability for Christine to rebuild her life with Krogstad can be accepted as a note of hope in Nora's case. Perhaps in the years to come, Nora and Torvald will also be able to restore their marriage.

Dr. Rank's function in the play also refers to a past occasion in Nora's life. Just as she used to seek the conversation of the maids as a refreshing change from the moralizing of her father, Nora finds amusement in Rank's companionship as a change from the tiresome cant of Torvald.

Rank's illness also serves as the physical counterpart of the moral illness of Krogstad, and by extension, of Helmer. An innocent victim of a social disease, the physician is as deeply concerned as Torvald in maintaining an exterior of well-being. Rather than allow anyone to witness the degrading aspects of his "final dissolution," Rank bids farewell to his friends and prepares to die in private. Torvald, by the same token, wishes to maintain appearances "at any cost" when he discover's Nora's disease of which he is the victim.

Torvald is shallow enough to be a mere foil for the character of Nora. Unfortunately, he is depicted with enough detail to appear a very plausible type of man, typical of many contemporary heads-of-the-family. He is a well-constructed social product, a proud specimen of a middle class husband. Because Nora has been so sheltered all her life, Torvald represents all the outside world she knows. Not only does he stand for the world of men and the world of business which has no place in her house-bound life, but he represents society at large, including all the community and legal ethics which do not concern her and religious ethics in which she has had no training. Ironically Ibsen sets up Torvald according to the same representation. For the author, Helmer stands for all the individual-denying social ills against which Ibsen has dedicated all his writing.

As a victim of his narrow view of society, Torvald inspires sympathy rather than reproach. When a man mistakes appearances for values, the basic blame must be attributed to his social environment. Ibsen, however, drives home the loathsome qualities of such a character by attributing to him a personal decadence. Implying that Torvald considers Nora merely an ornamented sex object, the author shows how he maintains amorous fantasies toward his wife: he dresses her as a Capri fisher girl and encourages her to dance in order to arouse his desires. As Helmer reinforces her girlish and immature ways, Ibsen implies an incest relationship, for Nora is made to observe that she was merely transferred from her father's tutelage to that of her husband without any change in her emotional life. It is with this final touch of perversion that Ibsen makes the character of Torvald thoroughly reprehensible to the audience.

Nora is by far the most interesting character in the play. Many critics have pointed out that such an immature, ignorant creature could never have attained the understanding and revolutionary qualities that Nora has at the time she leaves her home. Ibsen, however, has carefully constructed Nora so that her independence and far-sightedness have always shown through her adolescent capriciousness. Although her father and husband have seriously injured her practical education, Nora has retained enough native wisdom to confront an emergency. That she bungles the situation by a careless forgery provides further credence to her independence of thought as well as to her lack of sophistication. This mixture of wisdom and childishness is Nora's strongest quality. It enables her to oppose the knowledge of books and the doctrines of her worldly husband and to test by experience the social hypothesis which declares that duties to the family are the most sacred. Only an innocent creature can brave the perils of the outside world to find her identity.

Shocked audiences who objected to Nora's solution of her marital impasse and critics who considered her character unable to withstand the severe trial neglected to take account of the artistic truthfulness of the slammed door and its aftermath. One of the most common themes enduring in folklore and in less spontaneous works of art is this notion of the innocent journeying through the world to discover basic human values. The significance of these mythic themes is that only an innocent, fearless creature has the power of vision to see through the false values of sophisticated society. In Bunyan's *Pilgrim's Progress,* the story of Siegfried, Fielding's *Tom Jones,* and even in Thomas Mann's *The Magic Mountain,* we find the recurrent idea of youthful inquiry prevailing over worldly experience. Ibsen's Nora, though deriving from a much closer and realistic setting, is raised to a mythic level as she too accepts her inevitable quest, the sacred pursuit of her identity.

THEME

The interwoven themes of *A Doll's House* recur throughout most of Ibsen's works. The specific problem of this drama deals with the difficulty of maintaining an individual personality — in this case a feminine personality — within the confines of a stereotyped social role. The problem is personified as Nora, the doll, strives to become a self-motivated human being in a woman-denying man's world.

Refusing to be considered a feminist, Ibsen nevertheless expressed his view of a double-standard society. As he once forced a female character in an earlier play, *The Pillars of Society* to cry out, "Your society is a society of bachelor-souls!" he seems to have personified this male-oriented viewpoint by creating Torvald Helmer. In his notes for *A Doll's House,* Ibsen writes that the background of his projected drama "is an exclusively masculine society with laws written by men and with prosecutors and judges who regard feminine conduct from a masculine point of view." Since a woman is allegedly motivated out of love for her husband and children, it is unthinkable to her that laws can forbid acts inspired by affection, let alone punish their infraction. The outcome of this tension is that "the wife in the play is finally at her wit's end as to what is right and wrong"; she therefore loses her foothold in society and must flee the man who cannot dissociate himself from the laws of society. She can no longer live with a husband who cannot accomplish the "wonderful thing," a bridge of the mental gap which would bring his understanding and sympathies into agreement with her point of view.

It is quite impossible, however, to write a whole play with such a specific problem in mind. As characters and situations are formed by the dramatist's imagination, a more general, abstract thesis develops, with the specific problem becoming only a part of the whole. Thus *A Doll's House* questions the entire fabric of marital relationships, investigates the development of self-awareness in character, and eventually indicts all the false values of contemporary society which denies the worth of individual personality.

HEDDA GABLER

ACT I

Summary
After a six-months wedding trip, the bride and groom have returned home. Aunt Julia, Tesman's aunt, arrives to welcome them the following morning. As the curtain rises, the motherly old lady enters the well-furnished living room. She hands a bouquet of flowers to Bertha, the servant, who places them among the others which decorate the room at every corner. The aunt and the maid converse about the newlyweds, remarking with wonder and pride that the orphan nephew Miss Tesman raised is now a professor married to General Gabler's Daughter.

At this point George enters, greeting his aunt with warmth and affection. She inquires about the honeymoon, expecting to hear details of the romantic journey the young couple took touring southern Europe. Instead, Tesman delightedly recalls his tours through the archives and the collections of various libraries in order to gather research materials for his intended book, "The Domestic Industries of Brabant during the Middle Ages." His aunt, still curious, asks if George has "anything special" to tell her, if he has "any expectations," but Tesman merely answers that he expects to be appointed a professor. Aunt Julia mentions George's former colleague Eilert Lövborg. Despite publishing a recent book, she says, Lövborg has fallen a victim to his own misguided excesses. She is glad that her nephew's abilities will no longer be eclipsed by Lövborg's.

This brilliant but undisciplined young man was in love with Hedda some years ago, and they were close comrades. Confessing to her all his extravagant dissipations, his ambitions, the young man exposed his soul to this sheltered girl who was fascinated by a knowledge of life forbidden to her. When the friendship became serious, Hedda threatened Lövborg with her pistol, and he disappeared from her life from that moment on. George has no knowledge of his wife's former relationship with his friend.

The brief mention of Lövborg prefaces Hedda Gabler's entrance. She is tall and lovely, about twenty-eight years old, and responds coldly to the warmth of Miss Tesman's greeting. She is obviously bored by George's relatives, and shows no interest when her husband exclaims with pleasure over the pair of his old slippers Aunt Julia has brought him. Embroidered by Rina, the invalid sister of Miss Tesman, the slippers recall for George cherished memories of his childhood.

Hedda abruptly changes the subject, complaining that the servant has thrown her old bonnet on one of the chairs. The hat, however, belongs to Aunt Julia who has just purchased it in honor of George's bride. To overcome the embarrassment, Tesman hastily admires the bonnet, then bids his aunt admire Hedda's splendid appearance and to note how she has filled out from the journey. Angry, Hedda insists she looks the same as always, but Miss Tesman is enraptured at the implied pregnancy. Emotionally, she blesses Hedda Tesman "for George's sake." Promising to call each day, she takes her leave.

The maid announces an unexpected caller, a younger schoolmate of Hedda and a former acquaintance of George. Nervous and shy, Thea Elvsted explains the purpose of her visit. For the past year, Eilert Lövborg has lived in her house as tutor to her husband's children. The writer's conduct this past year has been irreproachable, Thea says, and he has managed to complete his successful new book while at the Elvsted's without once succumbing to temptation. Now that Lövborg has left their village, she is worried, for he has already remained a week "in this terrible town" without sending news of his whereabouts. Thea begs the Tesmans to receive him kindly if Eilert should visit them. Eager to extend hospitality to his former friend, George goes to write a letter of invitation.

Left alone with Thea, Hedda aggressively questions the reluctant younger woman, promising that they shall be close friends and address one another as "du." Thea admits that her marriage is not a happy one. She has nothing in common with her elderly husband who married her because it is cheaper to keep a wife rather than a housekeeper to look after the children.

Gaining confidence, Thea tells Hedda how a great friendship grew between Lövborg and herself until she gained an influence over him. "He never wrote anything without my assistance," she proudly declares; sharing Lövborg's work was the happiest time she has known all her life. The relationship means so much to her, that Thea has run away from home in order to live where Eilert Lövborg lives.

Yet her happiness is insecure, she tells Hedda. Although Lövborg had mentioned it only once, a woman's shadow stands between them. Hedda intently leans forward, eager to hear more. All that Lövborg said, Thea replies, is that this woman threatened to shoot him with a pistol when they parted. Mrs. Elvsted has heard about a red-haired singer whom Eilert used to visit, and she is especially worried now that this woman is in town again.

The maid announces Judge Brack, a family friend who has arranged George's affairs so that he could borrow money for his wedding trip and the villa that Hedda had set her heart on. A handsome mustached gentleman, carefully groomed and youthfully dressed, enters. About forty-five years old, Brack is very smooth in manner and bows gracefully when he and Thea are introduced.

The judge talks with Tesman about his debts while Hedda sees her guest to the door. When she returns, Brack announces his bad news: because Lövborg's book has been received so well, the writer might favorably compete for Tesman's promised professorship. George is thunderstruck, but Hedda shrugs indifferently. "There will be a sort of sporting interest in that," she says, and her husband apologizes for being unable to provide the necessities she expected: a liveried footman, a saddle horse, means for "going out into society." After Brack leaves, Hedda concludes wearily, "I shall have one thing at least to kill time with in the meanwhile — my pistols, George." She crosses to the next room, smiling coldly at her startled husband. "General Gabler's pistols!" she adds mockingly, and the curtain rings down.

Commentary

This first act, besides introducing characters, acquaints the audience with Hedda Gabler's surroundings in her new life as Mrs. Tesman. Brought up as a general's daughter accustomed to travel in aristocratic social circles, Hedda must confront her future as a housewife in a middle class household. The fact that she is pregnant reinforces her potential role as homemaker. The nature of her doom is underscored by the character of Miss Juliana Tesman who represents the older generation of domestic womanhood who has devoted her life to the care of others.

George Tesman, good natured and sentimental, assumes that the duty of a husband is merely to satisfy the domestic requirements of his wife so that she can be happy in the confines of her home. With this in mind, he agrees that they shall keep an open house — in

Hedda's chosen home—and maintain the luxuries important to proper entertaining. Believing that a woman naturally falls into household routines once she is married, George has no further insight into Hedda's temperament. Tesman's research into the "domestic industries of medieval Brabant" is an ironic symbol of his conservative, simple-minded views of married life, as well as a symbol that indicates his inability to encompass other than material details.

As to his heroine, Ibsen establishes her main symptoms of disaffection with life: a profound emotional coldness, an incapacity to interest herself in anything besides social pleasures, and a destructive desire to control the lives of others. Hedda cannot respond to the warmth of Aunt Julia, she cannot abide the idea of expecting a child, and was totally bored during her six-month wedding trip.

To further express her emotional sterility, Ibsen shows how Hedda is unable to reciprocate in a relationship. Like a young child, she can only receive without knowing how to give in return. Without reciprocating she accepts George's love and support; by pretending friendship, she learns all about Thea's personal life yet reveals no confidences of her own. Later on, when Lövborg recalls his previous relationship with Hedda, he describes how she extracted detailed confessions from him yet withheld her own self-revelations. This intense, almost morbid interest in the lives of others is another aspect of her empty emotional life. At the same time that investigating and analyzing other people's lives is one way for Hedda to gain some understanding of her own unsatisfied nature, she reveals her personal frigidity and adolescent self-centeredness.

This first act also demonstrates a pathological quality in Hedda's personality. Cruelly insulting Aunt Julia by complaining that it is the servant's bonnet lying in the chair, Hedda tries to undermine Miss Tesman's sense of worth. Compelling Thea to reveal her innermost feelings, she seems to search for Mrs. Elvsted's weaknesses so she can later use this knowledge for her own selfish purposes. Having established that his heroine is emotionally empty, yet eager to learn how other people face life's experiences, Ibsen shows how the imperious and unsubmissive Hedda tries to destroy the personal values of those whose satisfactions she cannot attain.

ACT II

Summary

As the curtain rises, Hedda is busy loading one of her pistols. There is nothing else to do besides shoot, she tells Judge Brack who has come to see Tesman. As they chat, Hedda tells him how bored she was during her wedding trip. She complains that her husband, with his everlasting talk about medieval civilization, is also boring. She is glad that Brack is a lively conversationalist who is "not at all a specialist." Her visitor wonders why Hedda accepted Tesman in the first place. "My day was done," she sighs. "I had positively danced myself tired, my dear judge." Besides, among all her suitors, George "who is correctness itself" was the one who offered marriage and a promising economic future; she saw no reason to refuse his proposal.

Brack, having himself been one of Hedda's admirers, admits that he never considered marriage. He enjoys being their family friend, he says, adding, "especially a friend of the mistress of the house." Very smoothly, he suggests that Hedda accept him as a third party in her domestic circle, for a "triangular friendship" will be convenient to all concerned. Hedda would then be able to enjoy the companionship of one who is not "a specialist" and Brack's relation with Tesman would continue as before. Hedda agrees without committing herself.

At this moment George enters. He has just visited his invalid Aunt Rina who is very sick, and he has brought some books, including the recent publication by Eilert Lövborg. Although Tesman expects to attend Brack's bachelor party this evening, he says he is eager to begin reading Lövborg's book and will come downstairs when it is time to leave. Hedda and the judge are free to continue their conversation.

Brack cannot understand why she is constantly bored; isn't she mistress of the very house she had set her heart on? She never liked this villa, replies Hedda. The matter came up when George escorted her home from a party one evening. As a pretext for conversation with the shy historian, Hedda relates, she pretended great interest in the villa they were just passing. This sham enthusiasm provided the first bond of sympathy between herself and Tesman; from this followed the courtship, engagement, and eventual marriage.

Brack observes that she requires a vocation as a relief from boredom. Hedda confesses she would like to try and push George into politics, but now that they have such meager finances this is impossible. Having the responsibility of a child would give her life an objective, Brack ventures. "No responsibilities for me," Hedda retorts angrily, and the judge remarks that her instincts are very unlike those of ordinary women. She despairs her purposeless life. "I often think there is only one thing in the world I have any turn for," Hedda observes darkly, " – boring myself to death."

Tesman, dressed for the dinner, comes to ask if Lövborg left any message. Don't expect him to join the party, Hedda says; he shall spend the evening with herself and Thea. At this moment, Lövborg enters. When they discuss his latest book, the writer denies its virtues, saying it is just a sop he threw to the critics. "This is the real book," he says drawing a packet from his coat, "the book I have put my true self into." Dealing with the "civilizing forces of the future," the manuscript excites George's curiosity and he is eager for Lövborg to read aloud from it. Tesman is further delighted when his friend promises not to compete with him for the professorship. The only interest Lövborg has in making his scheduled lecture tour, he tells George, is to accomplish a "moral victory." Refusing to drink a glass of punch with Brack and Tesman, Lövborg joins Hedda and she shows him the photograph album of their wedding journey. While she impersonally points out dull landscapes, Lövborg reminds her of the time when they were close comrades and he exposed all his secret thoughts to her. Her interest was not motivated by love, she admits, but by curiosity to learn about the outside world. "Comradeship in the thirst of life" could have continued even when they became serious lovers, Lövborg pursues. He regrets that she did not shoot him down as she threatened for he still finds her lovely and fascinating. I was afraid of a scandal, replies Hedda, and adds, "The fact that I dared not shoot you down—that was not my most arrant cowardice—that evening." Lövborg is filled with emotion. "Ah, Hedda! Hedda Gabler!" he murmurs. "Now I begin to see a hidden reason beneath our comradeship! You and I! After all, then, it was your craving for life—" and he understands that she was afraid to give herself in love.

Mrs. Elvsted appears and as they sit down together, Lövborg exclaims how courageous and lovely and inspiring Thea has been for him. When Lövborg refuses her offer of punch, Hedda subtly taunts him for feeling insecure about his temperance vow. She says that Tesman and Brack also noticed his lack of self-confidence. Again Lövborg refuses to drink, and Hedda turns smilingly to Thea. "You see," she says, "he is as firm as a rock." Thea needn't have run to her house, distracted with fear and worry about her friend's will power. Deeply injured at this lack of trust, Lövborg downs two cocktails in vengeance. Then he announces that he will, after all, join Tesman and Brack at this evening's dinner party.

Hedda assures them she will entertain Mrs. Elvsted until the writer returns to escort her home. When the men go out, Hedda comforts the agitated Thea. He will return at ten o'clock, she tells her friend. "I can see him already—flushed and fearless—with vine leaves in his hair." As the curtain falls, the victorious Hedda draws Thea, limp with exhaustion and anxiety, into the dining room for tea.

Commentary

In this act, Hedda fully expresses her desire to have power over someone. Frustrated at being unable to push her husband into a political career, incapable of maternal feelings, Hedda strives to compete with Thea for her influence over Lövborg. Having restored his liberty, she now looks forward to Eilert's fulfilling her romantic image of him as the incarnation of "the joy of life": he shall return "flushed and fearless with vine leaves in his hair!" That she has at once destroyed Thea's life work and Lövborg's morale is unimportant to Hedda; she merely wishes to have proof of her own worth by having power over someone.

At the same time that her craving for life distinguishes Hedda from "ordinary women," she shows, in this act, her deep commitment to the same bourgeois ethics which chain a woman to her domestic duties. Expressing to the judge that she accepted George Tesman because he "is correctness itself," Hedda implicitly rejects Brack's proposition of a domestic triangle: such a scandalous relationship would be repugnant to her. The judge, not recognizing that Hedda maintains such strict conventions, believes she has accepted his frank proposal.

Eilert Lövborg, however, shows more insight into Hedda's nature. When he accuses her of cowardice, he recognizes that she was too much a conformist to love an erratic and unconventional personality. Nevertheless at the time of their youthful friendship, Hedda expressed her "craving for life" by being fascinated by Eilert's intensity and brilliance; extracting detailed confessions from him was her way of vicariously experiencing a liberated and excessive way of life she was too afraid to live for herself.

ACT III

Summary

It is 7:00 the next morning. The ladies have been fitfully dozing during their nightwatch, and Hedda now sends Thea off for a good nap, promising to wake her when Lövborg arrives. When Tesman appears, Hedda is wide awake and listens eagerly as he tells her of Lövborg's extravagant behavior at the party. He was so drunk that he even dropped his manuscript without noticing, and George picked it up. Tesman praises his friend's book, admitting he feels envious for being himself unable to accomplish such brilliant work. Hedda demands the packet of papers, saying she would like to keep it awhile and read the manuscript.

At this moment George receives a telegram that his Aunt Rina is close to death. He rushes out, barely greeting Brack who has just arrived. The judge describes the rest of Eilert's activities. After the party, Lövborg landed at another soirée given by the red-haired singer, Mlle. Diana. Accusing her of robbing him, he caused such a disturbance that the police were called; to make matters worse, Lövborg resisted arrest by assaulting one of the officers.

Expecting Lövborg to seek Hedda's home as a refuge where he can meet with Mrs. Elvsted, Brack warns Hedda that he will resist any intrusion into the triangle; he wants nothing to threaten his free passage in and out of the Tesman residence. Hedda smiles mockingly at the implied threat. In other words, she calls to him as he goes, "you want to be the one cock in the basket."

When left alone, she takes the manuscript from the desk, but replaces it hastily at Lövborg's approach. Thea Elvsted emerges to greet the dishevelled writer. He has come, he sorrowfully says, to say their ways must part; from now on she must live her life without him. Thea implores him to allow her to experience her crowning satisfaction: to be with him when the book appears. There will be no book, he answers, for he destroyed the manuscript. It is as if he "killed a little child," she says in despair, and because the "child" belonged to her too, he had no right to destroy it. Thea can do nothing but return home, facing a life without any future, without any further meaning.

Alone with Hedda, Lövborg declares he is unable to try to rebuild his life. Worse than destroying the manuscript, which he had in his keeping like his own child, he just lost it during this night of "debauchery and riotness," he tells Hedda. Having so deeply failed Mrs. Elvsted, he has no future and will "only try and make an end of it all—the sooner the better." "Eilert Lövborg—listen to me," Hedda commands. She takes one of her pistols from its case and hands it to him. "Will you not try to—to do it beautifully?" she whispers. Thrusting the gun into his breast pocket, Lövborg leaves her.

Hedda, once more alone, takes the packet of papers from her desk. Sitting by the stove, she thrusts some pages into the fire. "Now I am burning your child, Thea!" she breathes. Peeling off papers, she hands them, one by one, into the flames until the entire manuscript is consumed. "Your child and Eilert Lövborg's," says Hedda with satisfaction. "I am burning—I am burning your child!"

Commentary

In this act, Hedda has confronted another frustration. Instead of seeing the awaited Lövborg rise to his full stature as a liberated artist, victoriously imbued with life's joy, she views a demoralized reveller who ruined the evening in a drunken orgy, facing, in addition, a possible jail sentence for assaulting a police officer.

Now that Thea has left the scene, however, she has one further chance of retaining her influence over Lövborg so that he will provide her with an act of "courage and freedom." Offering him the pistol, Hedda imagines that he will end his life bravely and romantically to accord with her favorite images of beauty enhanced by violence and death. Furthermore, the packet of papers she possesses represents a material hold she still has on Lövborg's destiny. By destroying the manuscript she had no share in creating or realizing, Hedda also kills the child she was unable to bear for Lövborg. By destroying that work of others which she should have accomplished herself, Hedda also destroys those constant reminders of her own inadequacies. Symbolically denying the life works of others, Hedda affirms her own unsatisfied sense of worth.

ACT IV

Summary

It is later in the evening. Miss Tesman enters, dressed in mourning. Hedda greets her, expressing regret for Rina's death. Aunt Julia plans to fill the gap in her life by finding someone to care for. Because it is necessary to live for someone, she says, she will seek an occupant for Rina's little room — some invalid in want of nursing.

After Julia leaves, George comes back, asking Hedda for the manuscript; he fears Lövborg might do himself injury before he can return it. Coolly, Hedda tells him she burned the papers. She wanted no one to put her husband "in the shade," she tells the delighted George, who never heard Hedda express her love for him.

Thea suddenly appears, apologizing for the intrusion. Having heard that Lövborg is in the hospital, she asks if they have further news of his condition. Brack, newly arrived, tells them that Lövborg wounded himself in the breast. "Not in the temple?" Hedda quickly inquires.

While Thea makes an effort to control herself, Hedda breaks the silence, declaring that there is beauty in this suicide for Eilert has made up his account with life. "He has had the courage to do the one right thing," she affirms.

Tesman expresses regret that Lövborg has left the world without bequeathing it "the book that would have immortalized his name." Mrs. Elvsted fumbles in her dress pocket. Producing many scraps of paper—"all the loose notes he used to dictate from"—she suggests that they might reconstruct the book. Tesman is delighted. Having spent his career organizing other people's manuscripts, he is eager to dedicate himself to putting together Lövborg's notes. Forgetful of everything but the papers spread on the table before them, Thea and George begin the task.

Hedda languidly reclines in the armchair, Judge Brack at her side. It gives her a new feeling of freedom, she tells her admirer, to know that a "deed of deliberate courage is still possible in this world —a deed of spontaneous beauty." Brack dispels her illusions, informing her of the true circumstances of Lövborg's death which he did not disclose to Thea. Lövborg did not die voluntarily, he tells the astonished Hedda. The police discovered the body in Mlle. Diana's boudoir, Lövborg had forced his way into the singer's apartment, talking wildly about a "lost child." While they struggled, the pistol in his breast pocket discharged itself, and he died from a bullet wound in his bowels.

Her shocked face is disfigured by an expression of loathing and despair. "Oh, what a curse is it that makes everything I touch turn ludicrous and mean?" she cries out. Brack remains unperturbed. One more disagreeable aspect remains, he says, for Lövborg must have stolen the pistol. Hedda passionately denies this, and Brack nods. He says that if someone were to identify the pistol, she herself would be drawn into the scandal. "So I am in your power, Judge Brack," says Hedda. "You have me at your beck and call from this time forward." Leaning closer, he assures her that he shall not "abuse his advantage."

Hedda stands behind Mrs. Elvsted, passing her hands affectionately through her friend's hair. "Here you are, Thea, sitting with Tesman—just as you used to sit with Eilert Lövborg," and she asks whether she can inspire George as well as she used to inspire Eilert. Intently working, her husband exclaims that he begins to feel inspired by Thea, and asks his wife to return to Judge Brack. "Is there nothing I can do to help you two?" asks Hedda. "No, nothing in the world," George answers without looking up.

He suggests to Thea that she rent the room in Aunt Julia's apartment; without disturbing Hedda they can meet there every evening to work on the manuscript. "But how am I to get through the evenings out here?" Hedda calls from the back room. Tesman assures her that the judge shall look in on her every now and then. Brack gaily adds that he shall visit "every blessed evening," and that "we shall get on capitally together, we two!" Loud and clear, Hedda answers, "Yes, don't you flatter yourself we will, Judge Brack. Now that you are the one cock in the basket—" A shot rings out. Tesman, Mrs. Elvsted, and Brack discover Hedda stretched lifeless on the sofa; she had shot herself in the temple.

Commentary

Going beyond the destruction that Hedda began in the previous acts, circumstances depicted in the final scene destroy the life's work of each other character. Julia's sister dies, leaving the old aunt with no one to care for; Tesman relinquishes his work on medieval Brabant; Thea has definitely lost Lövborg; and Hedda confronts profound disillusion when she learns of Eilert's ignoble death.

The secondary characters, however, all find vocational rebirth as they confront their ruined life purposes. Thea, having saved Lövborg's notes, begins, with George Tesman, to conceive a new "child"; the professor so expert at assembling other people's manuscripts can dedicate his abilities to reconstruct his dead friend's brilliant ideas; and Julia can again care for her beloved nephew now that Hedda is gone.

Hedda alone faces a life without a future. Deprived of her satisfaction at the beauty of Eilert's suicide, she learns that she was in fact responsible for the abhorrent manner of Lövborg's death. Her ideal of freedom, courage and beauty turns into a loathsome reality. Judge Brack applies the final vulgar touch to a situation that Hedda already finds repulsive; he alone can inform the police of the facts that would implicate her in a shocking scandal. The conventional Hedda must either succumb to Brack's power or face a public inquiry. Now that even her husband has no further need of her, no one depends upon Hedda at this point. On the other hand she is unwillingly enthralled by the ruthless Brack. Deprived of freedom, Hedda faces either "boring herself to death" or committing a valiant suicide.

GENERAL ANALYSIS OF *HEDDA GABLER*

INTRODUCTION

Written in 1890, *Hedda Gabler* is a high point in Ibsen's creative life. Although the "social dramas" of his prose period depict full-bodied and believable characters, Ibsen achieved a psychological depth in *Hedda Gabler* that his later works never surpassed. Having investigated the feminine character in a male-oriented society in *Doll's House* and *Ghosts,* Ibsen enlarged his scrutiny to encompass the full pathology of the social female. Although Hedda Gabler is an example of perverted femininity, her situation illuminates what Ibsen considered to be a depraved society, intent on sacrificing to its own self-interest the freedom and individual expression of its most gifted members.

CHARACTERIZATION OF SECONDARY CHARACTERS

As usual in Ibsen's tightly constructed dramas, each character provides, by comparison, insight into every other character. The characterizations of Thea Elvsted and Miss Juliana Tesman, unlike Hedda, depict women who submit to their socially-imposed feminine roles and derive satisfaction from their lives: they devote themselves to the unselfish tasks of raising children and serving to inspire masculine creativity. Julia, for instance, has raised George Tesman who became a promising academician, and now that the nephew has grown up, she takes care of her invalid sister. Thea, after having married an unloving elderly man in order to care for his household, has found a satisfying life assisting and inspiring the work of a creative and brilliant writer. Through her devotion, Lövborg has been able to channel his undisciplined energies to produce according to his potential. His masterpiece, the product of their mutual inspiration, is the natural child which, through love, Thea and Eilert have conceived.

Compared to Aunt Julia and Mrs. Elvsted, Hedda seems an unnatural woman. Refusing to relinquish her freedom, she regards childbearing as loathsome and destroys the manuscript conceived by Thea and Lövborg as if she were murdering her own child. Degrading Aunt Julia by insulting her new bonnet, Hedda expresses hostility toward her husband as well as his relatives.

Hedda's emotional sterility is counterparted by Judge Brack's lack of compassion. Unlike Hedda, Brack has a profession and is free to amuse himself without overstepping the masculine social conventions. This parallel between them illustrates the double standards of society which denies rights of self-expression to women.

The emptiness of Brack's emotional life is underscored by his attributes of vulgarity and lechery. Willing to first compromise Hedda's respectability as a married woman, he has no compunctions about using blackmail as a weapon guaranteeing his selfish ends. Like Hedda, Brack wishes to substitute power over someone for love which he is unable to give.

Tesman's bumbling ordinariness contrasts vividly and humorously with Lövborg's flamboyant and creative brilliance. Where George writes about the "domestic industries of Brabant in the middle ages", Eilert works on a book dealing with the "civilizing forces" of humanity in the future. Tesman delights in researching among old manuscripts, while Lövborg considers the problems of the future.

Seeing only an inexperienced bride, the husband admires Hedda for her qualities of beauty and poise and expects that she will learn to love him at some future time. Hedda's former lover, on the other hand, is fascinated by her "craving for life" and has insight into her cowardly retreat to convention. Tesman is eager for his professional appointment which will guarantee his ability to support his household, while Lövborg looks forward to the "moral victory" he will achieve from delivering his scheduled lectures. Solicitous to his aunts, Tesman cherishes sentimental reminders of the love and care he received as a child (as shown by his delight at receiving an old pair of slippers Rina embroidered for him); Lövborg, recognizing that the past is irreclaimable, breaks with Thea when he loses the manuscript they have written together.

Ibsen sets the brilliant writer as an exact counterpart to the medieval scholar in many ways. Where one is erratic, the other is steady; one deals with abstract and philosophical problems, the other concerns himself with concrete and detailed minutiae. Because of these qualities, however, Lövborg, a representation of the discontinuity in living a free life, cannot carry on his work. Tesman, on the other hand, representing the continuity of living a structured life, is able to take up Lövborg's work and eventually fulfill the writer's promise of greatness. With this situation, Ibsen seems to imply a balance of human forces: the erratic genius is necessary to provide the impelling idea, but the character who is gifted with less imagination and an ability to work hard at concrete details is the one able to realize the idea.

CHARACTERIZATION OF HEDDA GABLER

Placed in similar crises as previous Ibsen heroines, Hedda Gabler faces an impasse in her life. Sharing Nora's craving for freedom, and Mrs. Alving's compliance with social conventions, Hedda finds no outlet for her personal demands; she is constantly torn between her aimless desire for freedom and her commitment to standards of social appearance. Refusing to submit to her womanly destiny, Hedda has such an unsatisfied craving for life that she is incapable of being emotionally involved with others.

When Nora Helmer recognized her own unsatisfied needs, she left her husband and children. Considering her most "sacred duty" was to find herself, she left home to discover her personal worth through facing life's experiences before being able to relate to others. Like Nora, Hedda Gabler is a stranger to herself. However, lacking Nora's daring and defiance of conventions, she is unable to undergo the trials of self-evaluation and becomes a morbidly self-vindictive, destructive virago, capable only to strike out against the successful socially conforming individuals who represent an implicit reproach to her uninformed cravings. In the play, Ibsen provides enough information to show how Hedda's problem is the product of her special background.

Raised by her military father, Hedda must have grown up in an atmosphere of strict discipline and conformity to rules. Becoming a beautiful sought-after young woman, she attended many social affairs but never found anyone to marry; probably she was not rich enough to interest the eligible bachelors of high social standing.

As a product of the nineteenth century, where women were destined to become either respectable old maids like George's aunts, or humble housekeepers like Mrs. Elvsted, Hedda is an anomaly. Instead of preparing his daughter for wifehood or motherhood, General Gabler taught her to ride and shoot, skills symbolic of the military mystique which became for Hedda the basis of her fascination with the violent and the romantic. Inheriting from her father, whose forbidding portrait hangs in the Tesman's drawing room, his pride and coldness as well as his imperious commanding attitude toward others of a lower rank, Hedda lacks compassion for weak and submissive creatures like Thea and Aunt Julia but has a respect for power and independence, qualities she finds in Brack and Lövborg.

Since it was unthinkable at the time for a woman to receive either an intellectual or a professional education, Hedda's intelligence remained stultified. Unable to recognize the demands of her individuality, she remains enslaved to a standard of social conventionality and can only admire from afar the forbidden world where there is freedom of expression and an uninhibited exuberance of life. Eilert Lövborg provides Hedda with the vicarious experience of an individual who enjoys an unfettered creative life. She drew sustenance from his soul's outpourings as he told her of his dreams, his work, and his excessive way of life. At the same time, Hedda was too ignorant and inexperienced to accurately, evaluate Lövborg's character; she regarded him not as a creature of reality, but as the person — and realization of her adolescent quest for the romantic. When Lövborg made serious demands on her, Hedda rejected him. Stultified at the emotional level of an adolescent and repelled by his unconventionality, she could no longer tolerate the intensity of an actual relationship and shrank from responding to his demands.

George Tesman, on the other hand, is an acceptable husband especially because he makes no demands on Hedda's emotional incapacity. Posing no threat to her internal security, he is able to provide her with material security and to indulge her tastes for luxury and an active social life. Besides being sincerely fond of his bride, Tesman satisfies Hedda's conventional standards (he is "correctness itself") and leaves her imagination free to indulge her demand for independence and courage.

Having thus married to innure herself from any internal threats, l.edda coldly plans to base her life on the enjoyment of external advantages. The drama begins at this point, and develops characters and events which swiftly undermine Hedda's system of values. Her pregnancy is the first disturbance to her calculated system of inner protection. Hedda then learns that Tesman's appointment may be deferred, a situation which deprives her of luxury and active social entertainments.

It is significant that Lövborg, Hedda's romantic ideal of the free and life-intoxicated hero, becomes George's professional rival. According to her conception, Eilert's free spirit must have somehow been conquered, or she must have deceived herself as to his true nature. In either case, Hedda is deprived of her favorite ideal and must try to reinstate the old Lövborg in order to maintain an equilibrium between fantasy and reality. When she discovers that Thea Elvsted has preempted her former power over Eilert, now temperate, hard-working, and successful, she overrides Thea to gain the desired influence over Lövborg. This too backfires, for his liberation from Thea's steadying influence becomes a sordid debauchery that ends with Eilert's ignoble death. Thus, all Hedda's expectations dissolve into a vulgar residue that she cannot accept.

Brack administers the final blow to her dream of independence when he threatens her with blackmail. After all her efforts at manipulating others so that she can remain free of fettering responsibilities and slavish domestic attachments, Hedda learns that she is forever at Brack's "beck and call" if she wishes to avoid being involved in a sordid scandal. With this final disillusion, Hedda no longer has a life worth facing. In a tragic attempt to "do it beautifully" she puts a bullet through her temple.

CONCLUSION

The problem of Hedda Gabler illuminates the universal problem of woman in a society built by men. Like Mrs. Alving and Nora Helmer, Hedda must make an independent decision about her life. Women, however, in all but the most progressive societies, are barred from participating in the world outside their households and are not equipped for independence outside their families. Thus, Hedda Gabler, despite a profound craving for independence, has no personal resources with which to realize self-responsibility. Having the desire, but not the ability, for a constructive effort at self determination, she becomes a modern Medea, expressing her frustration in destructive attempts at self-realization. Not having any positive influence in the world, Hedda Gabler can only define herself negatively: she destroys what she cannot accept. Undermining her husband with her coldness, denying her pregnancy, destroying Thea's life-work. burning Lövborg's creative product, ruining the child-manuscript, and finally, committing suicide, are all perverted attempts to satisfy her "craving for life." By depicting the pathology of a frustrated woman in *Hedda Gabler,* Ibsen declares his most powerful protest against the double standard society.

DRAMA OF IBSEN

Although the plays are interesting for their social message, sen's dramas would not survive today were it not for his consummate skill as a technician. Each drama is carefully wrought into a tight logical construction where characters are clearly delineated and interrelated, and where events have a symbolic as well as actual significance. The symbolism in Ibsen's plays is rarely overworked. Carefully integrated to unify the setting, events, and character portrayals, the symbols are incidental and subordinate to the truth and consistency of his picture of life.

Having been interested in painting as a youth, Ibsen was always conscious of making accurate observations. As a dramatist, he considered himself a photographer as well, using his powers of observation as a lens, while his finished plays represented the proofs of a skilled darkroom technician. The realism of his plays, the credibility of his characters, the immediacy of his themes attest to these photographic skills at which Ibsen so consciously worked. Among his countless revisions for each drama, he paid special heed to the accuracy of his dialogue. Through constant rewriting, he brought out the maximum meaning in the fewest words, attempting to fit each speech into the character of the speaker. In addition, Ibsen's ability as a poet contributed a special beauty to his terse prose.

The problems of Ibsen's social dramas are consistent throughout all his works. Georg Brandes, a contemporary critic, said of Ibsen, as early as the 1860's, that "his progress from one work to the other is not due to a rich variety of themes and ideas, but on the contrary to a perpetual scrutiny of the same general questions, regarded from different points of view." In *A Doll's House,* he especially probed the problems of the social passivity assigned to women in a male-oriented society. After considering the plight of Nora Helmer, he then investigated what would happen had she remained at home. The consequence of his thoughts appear in *Ghosts.* Going one step further, Ibsen investigated the fallacies inherent in his own idealism. Much as Pastor Manders applies empty principles to actual situations, Gregers Werle is shown trying to impose an idealistic viewpoint when circumstances demand that individuals can only accept their lives by clinging to "life lies." Although *The Wild Duck* differs in treatment from *Hedda Gabler,* the plays both have protagonists who find in their imaginations an outlet for their frustrations. *Hedda Gabler,* however, with its emphasis on individual psychology, is a close scrutiny of a woman like Nora Helmer or Mrs. Alving who searches for personal meaning in a society which denies freedom of expression.

Professor Koht sums up the dramatist's investigations:

The thing which filled [Ibsen's] mind was the individual man, and he measured the worth of a community according as it helped or hindered a man in being himself. He had an ideal standard which he placed upon the community and it was from this measuring that his social criticism proceeded.

Secondary to, and in connection with, his idea that the individual is of supreme importance, Ibsen believed that the final personal tragedy comes from a denial of love. From this viewpoint we see that Torvald is an incomplete individual because he attaches more importance to a crime against society than a sin against love. The same is true for Pastor Manders. Hedda Gabler is doomed to a dissatisfied life because she too is unable to love, and Hedvig's tragic suicide is the result of her pathetic attempt to recall her father's affections. In Ibsen's other plays, particularly *Brand,* this theme is of primary importance.

In an age where nations were striving for independence, Ibsen's sense of democracy was politically prophetic. He believed, not that "right" was the prerogative of the mass majority, but that it resided among the educated minority. In the development and enrichment of the individual, he saw the only hope of a really cultured and enlightened society.

IBSEN'S CONTRIBUTIONS TO THE THEATER

Until the latter part of the nineteenth century, theater remained a vehicle of entertainment. Insights into the human condition were merely incidental factors in the dramatist's art. Ibsen, however, contributed a new significance to drama which changed the development of modern theater. Discovering dramatic material in everyday situations was the beginning of a realism that novelists as different as Zola and Flaubert were already exploiting. When Nora quietly confronts her husband with "Sit down, Torvald, you and I have much to say to each other," drama became no longer a mere diversion, but an experience closely impinging on the lives of the playgoers themselves. With Ibsen, the stage became a pulpit, while the dramatist exhorting his audience to reassess the values of society, became the minister of a new social responsibility.

COMPLETE LIST OF IBSEN'S DRAMAS

VERSE 1850 Catiline
1850 The Vikings Barrow
1853 St. John's Night
1855 Lady Inger of Ostraat
1856 The Feast of Solhaug
1857 Olaf Liljekraus
1858 Vikings of Helgeland
1862 Love's Comedy
1864 The Pretenders
1866 Brand
1867 Peer Gynt
1869 The League of Youth (prose)
1873 Emperor and Galilean (blank verse)

PROSE 1877 Pillars of Society
1879 A Doll's House
1881 Ghosts
1882 Enemy of the People
1884 The Wild Duck
1886 Rosmersholm
1888 The Lady from the Sea
1890 Hedda Gabler
1892 The Master Builder
1894 Little Eyolf
1896 John Gabriel Borkman
1900 When We Dead Awaken

SELECTED BIBLIOGRAPHY

Brian W. Downs, *A Study of Six Plays by Ibsen;* Cambridge, England: 1950.

Edmund Gosse, *Henrik Ibsen.*

Halvdan Koht, *The Life of Ibsen,* translated by R. L. McMahon and H. A. Larsen; 2 vols.; New York: 1931.

Janko Lavrin, *Ibsen, An Approach;* London, 1950.

M. S. Moses, *Henrik Ibsen, the Man and His Plays;* Boston: 1920.

George Bernard Shaw, *The Quintessence of Ibsenism;* Ayot St. Lawrence edition, vol. 19; London: 1921.

Hermann J. Wiegand, *The Modern Ibsen,* New York: 1925.

Adolph Edouard Zucker, *Ibsen, the Master Builder;* New York: 1929.

SAMPLE EXAMINATION QUESTIONS

1. Using specific examples, discuss how Ibsen's "progress from one work to the other" is due to a "perpetual scrutiny of the same general questions regarded from different points of view."

2. Do you feel that Ibsen's drama is "dated"? To defend your view, cite dramatic themes in these plays which you consider to be universal, or limited in scope.

3. Why does Ibsen choose a woman as his protagonist in these plays?

4. At least one character in each play prefers his imaginary view of life to a realistic viewpoint. With this in mind, discuss the life-views of Torvald Helmer and Hedda Gabler.

5. In what ways do the vocations of Torvald Helmer and George Tesman provide additional insight into their character?

6. In each play, show how the first act forewarns the audience of almost all the forthcoming events in the rest of the drama.

7. Point out some instances where Ibsen is able to "externalize" inner problems by using effective symbols.

8. Devise an alternative ending for *A Doll's House* trying not to violate Ibsen's dramatic thesis. Defend either your new conclusion or the inviolability of Ibsen's original ending.

9. Explain the symbolic significance of hereditary disease in *A Doll's House*.

10. Why is *Hedda Gabler* rather than *Hedda Tesman* the title of the drama?

11. What is the symbolic value ascribed to Hedda's pistol.

12. Why is it dramatically necessary for Hedda Gabler to burn Lövborg's manuscript?

NOTES

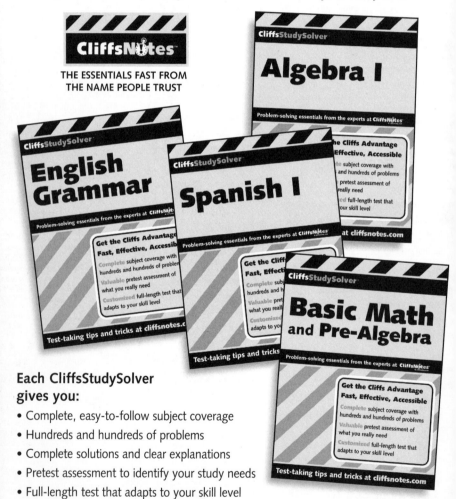